JOBS IN THE U.S. ARMY

Published in 2023 by The Rosen Publishing Group, Inc.
29 East 21st Street, New York, NY 10010

Portions of this work were originally authored by Earle Rice Jr. and published as *Careers in the U.S. Army*. All new material in this edition was authored by Eric Ndikumana.

Cataloging-in-Publication Data

Names: Ndikumana, Eric.
Title: Jobs in the U.S. Army / Eric Ndikumana.
Description: New York : Rosen Publishing, 2023. | Series: Exploring military careers | Includes glossary and index.
Identifiers: ISBN 9781499469929 (pbk.) | ISBN 9781499469936 (library bound) | ISBN 9781499469943 (ebook)
Subjects: LCSH: United States. Army--Juvenile literature. | United States. Army--Vocational guidance--Juvenile literature.
Classification: LCC UA25.N355 2023 | DDC 355.00973--dc23

Some of the images in this book illustrate individuals who are models. The depictions do not imply actual situations or events.

Manufactured in the United States of America

CPSIA Compliance Information: Batch #CSRYA23. For further information, contact Rosen Publishing, New York, New York, at 1-800-237-9932.

Find us on

CONTENTS

CHAPTER 1

GROWING THE GROUND FORCE

The U.S. Army has a history as old as the United States itself. Though the modern army has undergone many changes over its centuries-long history, one thing has not changed: the branch's commitment to defending the country through the deployment of ground troops and land-based weaponry. Army soldiers have fought in countless conflicts, protecting peace both at home and abroad when called upon.

A set of principles called the Warrior Ethos is essential for the 21st-century soldier. Beginning as early as boot camp training, army soldiers are taught the four ideas of the Warrior Ethos, to which they must adhere:

- I will always place the mission first.
- I will never accept defeat.
- I will never quit.
- I will never leave a fallen comrade.

Soldiers live by these words, internalizing them until they can be recited from memory. By following the Warrior Ethos, members of the army learn how to become better fighters, better friends, and better citizens. Army soldiers are behind some of the U.S. military's most courageous stories.

THE BIRTH OF THE ARMY

The U.S. Army is the same age as the United States it was created to defend. In 1760, George III claimed the throne of Great Britain and Ireland. At the time, the Seven Years' War (1756–1763)—known in North America as the French and Indian War—was still raging. After its conclusion, the new king found himself facing a huge debt because of the war. To regain financial power, the British government launched a series of new and increased taxes in North America. Colonists, angry at these new changes and increasingly hungry for independence, started to raise and train citizen militias. By the spring of 1775, colonial America had reached open rebellion.

Needless to say, the British were not pleased with the new developments across the sea. On April 14, 1775, General Thomas Gage was ordered to seize militia arms stockpiled in Concord, Massachusetts. Gage was the British commander in chief in North America; he was also the governor of the Massachusetts colony. Gage sent 700 soldiers to destroy the stash of arms.

During their march to Concord, British soldiers engaged and defeated a group from the small Massachusetts militia known as "minutemen" at Lexington on April 19, 1775. This nickname came from their reported ability to assemble for battle quickly—with a minute's notice. When they arrived at Concord, the British met a larger force of minutemen. The British were forced to march back to Boston, leaving their mission unfulfilled. In these short battles, the shots "heard round the world" had been fired: the American Revolution had begun.

King George III was the ruler of Britain during the time of the American Revolution.

The American Revolution began with a bang, as the colonists clashed with the British at Lexington and Concord.

Before long, militia groups from all over New England laid siege to Boston. Their assault would not stop for almost a year. Meanwhile, the Continental Congress—the main colonial law-making body at the time—unified the colonial militias as the Continental Army on June 14, 1775. Congress selected George Washington to lead the army. Washington, a Virginia soldier and planter, became the U.S. Army's first commander in chief.

Though Washington accepted the command, he was hesitant to do so. He believed that he was unequal to the huge task of leading his soldiers to victory against the British. However, after he took the position, he quickly warmed up to the challenge. He rightly assessed that he and the army had a chance to change the course of history and create a nation the likes of which had never been seen. Under his steady leadership, the United States emerged victorious. After the fighting, Washington went on to serve two terms as the first U.S. president.

The Continental Army was a unique military force at the time. It was mostly made up of long-term volunteers. Its size ranged roughly from 5,000 to 20,000 troops. Soldiers sometimes had to supply their own uniforms. Most men wore work or hunting

WASHINGTON WINS

The American Revolution stretched across eight years. Early on, Congress had favored trying to win the war by risking everything in a single large battle. Washington disagreed. He knew that the colonies needed more time to build and train an army that would be strong enough to go toe-to-toe with the British. In the autumn of 1776, Washington changed the risky American strategy of taking a chance on a single large-scale battle to draw out the conflict. This strategic change bought the time the nation needed to build a strong army. The Continental Army wore down the British over time, and America won its independence. After the war ended, the army was disbanded.

The Continental Army owed much of its early success to the leadership of George Washington, the first great American general.

clothes. Washington himself wore the blue and buff of the Virginia militia, but green and brown became the main uniform colors because those dyes were most available. Blue did not become the official color until 1779.

Regulars of the Continental Army were commonly reliable and surprisingly well trained. Foot soldiers wielded smoothbore muskets with bayonets and American long rifles. Many carried hatchets, a weapon adopted from Native Americans. Cavalry was almost never used. Cannons used to support the infantry included 3- to 24-pounders and 5.5- and

8-inch (14 and 20 cm) howitzers. A few 18-, 24-, and 32-pounder siege guns were also available.

During the Revolution, the Continental Army fought British and Hessian regulars in European-style combat. This traditional, orderly style of fighting was almost unrecognizable compared to the wild style of colonial militias. Over the years, tactics evolved. Fighting styles grew into a blend of British linear formations and frontier-style fighting from hidden positions.

The Continental Army set the standard for U.S. infantry troops. Similarly, George Washington became the model for future U.S. military officers.

A BROADER MISSION

Though the Continental Army was disbanded at the end of the war, the nation still needed fighters. Congress established the Army of the Constitution in 1789. Congress wanted this new fighting force to meet the needs of a young nation, especially regarding defense and policing of the frontier. The Army of the Constitution grew out of the first permanent U.S. Army, which was formed in 1784 under the Articles of Confederation. The Articles were the first national constitution of the independent United States. This tiny force of regulars and militia numbered about 800 officers and enlisted men. Its size grew and shrunk as needed to meet and resolve conflicts.

In 1794, President Washington sent General "Mad Anthony" Wayne to put down a Native American uprising near the modern city of Toledo, Ohio. Wayne defeated the Native Americans in the Battle of Fallen Timbers, which lasted less than an hour. It began with a cavalry attack, a tactic previously rarely used, and ended with a bayonet charge. In 1795, the ensuing Treaty of Greenville forced the Native Americans to give up land to the United States. The treaty also served to end British influence in the region.

EARLY PRESIDENTS AND THE ARMY

In 1797, John Adams took George Washington's place as president, and Washington returned to Virginia. In 1801, Thomas Jefferson became the third U.S. president. The previous armies fielded by the United States had variable sizes, but Jefferson wanted to keep things steady. He fixed the size of the peacetime army at two regiments of infantry and one of artillery, plus a small corps of engineers. The army's total strength stood at just under 3,300 men.

Jefferson's influence on the army did not stop there. In 1802, Congress authorized Jefferson to establish the U.S. Military Academy at West Point, New York. The school's primary mission was to train engineering officers for the army. It opened on July 4, 1802.

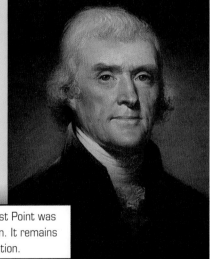

The U.S. Military Academy at West Point was established by President Jefferson. It remains a highly respected learning institution.

FIGHTING THE BRITISH—AGAIN

Just a few decades after gaining independence from Britain, the United States found itself in the War of 1812 with its former mother country. Though Americans were hesitant to enter another conflict, war seemed to be the only option in the face of unfair British practices as it warred with France. Britain repeatedly violated the marine rights of neutral nations. American efforts to gain control of Canadian lands did little to calm the waters of mutual discontent.

The War of 1812 brought major changes to the army. Its strength was authorized to grow to more than 60,000. Though enlistment numbers fell far short of maximum allowed, the army's performance greatly improved as battle-seasoned officers rose to middle and high ranks. Famous among the new senior officer corps was Winfield Scott. He would later become the commanding general of the army. After the War of 1812 showed that European powers were not content to leave the young United States in peace, the army's new mission was to gain strength to better protect the nation from rulers across the sea.

Under presidents James Madison and James Monroe, the army established permanent general staff bureaus and official regulations for uniforms. Though these changes seem small, they helped improve the army's management and operations. The army also constructed a system of coastal forts. Around the same time, Captain Sylvanus Thayer refreshed the U.S. Military Academy. The school had originally suffered under poor administration. Thayer first championed a strict code of discipline, then instituted a four-year curriculum focused on engineering and mathematics education.

NATIVE AMERICAN ENGAGEMENTS

In 1821, Congress reduced the size of the army again. It was now to be made up of 11 line regiments. These standing troops were supported by several general staff bureaus. The bureaus included quartermaster, engineers, ordnance, medical, and subsistence. Each bureau reported to the commanding general of the army. For the next two decades, the army was a key asset to the government as it started to truly construct the nation. It helped develop and expand the new United States. The army also played a key role in Native American management and relocation.

Winfield Scott, now a brigadier general, continued his rise to power in the 1830s. Scott commanded U.S. forces in the Black Hawk War in 1832. He also took part in the war against the Seminole Native Americans in 1836. Two years later, he was responsible for the removal of the Cherokee from South Carolina, Georgia, and Tennessee. On July 5, 1841, Major General Winfield Scott was named commanding general of the army.

SOUTH OF THE BORDER

In 1845, the United States annexed Texas. By this time, the country had embraced the concept of Manifest Destiny. The concept referred to what Americans believed was their right to spread across the entire continent. In 1846, war broke out with Mexico over disputed territory claims in Texas. At first, Winfield Scott supported General Zachary Taylor's campaigns in Texas and northern Mexico. Scott eventually changed his mind, arguing that a direct assault on Mexico City would bring a quick end to the war. Scott personally took command of the campaign in southern Mexico.

General Winfield Scott contributed to many of the U.S. Army's early victories.

Scott was at the head of an American invasion force in an unopposed landing at Vera Cruz in March 1847. Under his leadership, the army then began the long walk to Mexico City. Many officers of future fame served under him, including Ulysses S. Grant and Robert E. Lee, among others.

In Mexico, Americans fought several key battles against the forces of General Antonio López de Santa Anna. The two nations battled at Jalapa, Cerro Gordo, Contreras, Churubusco, Chapultepec, and Mexico City. Under Scott, the Americans won every single battle. He was one of the army's first truly great tactical minds.

In early 1848, the Treaty of Guadalupe Hidalgo brought an end to the Mexican-American War, a victory for the United States earned almost entirely by the army. As part of the terms of the treaty, Mexico gave up a huge amount of land to the United States, including the areas that would eventually become Arizona, California, Nevada, New Mexico, and Utah. In addition to increasing the nation's land size, the army's series of victories proved to the world that there was a new continental power to fear: the United States of America.

CHAPTER 2

INFIGHTING AND MOVING WEST

After the end of the Mexican-American War, the United States entered a time of rapid westward expansion. As the country grew in size, its armed force grew in strength—and responsibility. U.S. Army soldiers dressed in blue coats provided protection for settlers in the West, acting almost as a strong police force in the vast open spaces now available to Americans. Many of the army's engagements during the early 1800s were with Native Americans; more than 20 smaller-scale wars were fought in the new U.S. territories. The army's size increased to meet these new supervisory tasks, but after a brief time of relative peace out West, the nation would soon be fighting against itself: North against South.

A HOUSE DIVIDED

In 1861, a civil war broke out in the young nation. Northerners and Southerners disagreed on the political and economic issues of states' rights, trade and tariffs, and—most importantly—slavery. Abraham Lincoln's 1860 election as president only increased tensions, as Lincoln was known to be opposed to slavery. Soon after his election, 7 (eventually 11) Southern states left the Union. They formed the Confederate States of America under President Jefferson Davis.

Lincoln's election to the post of president pushed some Southern states to secede, fearing that he would end the use of slave labor.

On April 12, 1861, the Confederates fired on and later seized Fort Sumter, South Carolina. The rebel cannon fire marked the beginning of the American Civil War. President Lincoln countered swiftly. Just weeks before the war began, he made a vow to reclaim and defend all federal property and places within Confederate territory. He intended to keep this pledge, and he gave the army the task of preserving the Union.

In 1861, at the outset of the Civil War, the Union Army numbered just over 16,000 men. The Confederacy came into the war with an army of about 35,000 men. President Lincoln quickly responded to the attack on Fort Sumter. He called for 75,000 volunteers to join up and put down the Southern revolt. The rallying cry worked, and new army volunteers numbered closer to 100,000.

In three months, the Union Army grew to more than 200,000 men. By war's end in 1865, the blue-clad Union Army would field almost a million fighters. In Confederate gray, however, stood 750,000 soldiers who would oppose them. For the first time in nearly its 100-year history, the army was forced to face a crisis of loyalty. Roughly one-quarter of its officer corps resigned to support the Confederacy. Both sides had to resort to a draft to maintain troop levels. The more heavily populated North benefitted from having more people to call on.

In July 1861, Union forces marched toward Richmond, Virginia, the Confederate capital. Before they arrived, Confederate troops defeated them at Bull

Brother fought brother during the Civil War. Confederate soldiers wanted to defend their way of life, and Union soldiers wanted to abolish slavery.

Run Creek. The South claimed the first victory of the Civil War, forcing the Union soldiers to retreat back toward Washington, D.C.

Northern forces, commanded by General Ulysses S. Grant, began the first major campaign in the western theater in 1862. Grant's victories at Fort Donelson in Tennessee restored Northern belief in the army. After he called for the enemy to give up the battle, his harsh terms earned him the nickname "Unconditional Surrender," a play on his first two initials. Grant followed his Donelson successes with a major victory at Shiloh, Tennessee.

In the East, General Robert E. Lee and the Army of Northern Virginia won several victories in the Seven Days' Battle near Richmond. Lee then lost at Antietam Creek, near Sharpsburg, Maryland. He would bounce back to defeat General Ambrose Burnside's Union Army of the Potomac at Fredericksburg, Virginia, in December 1862. Lee secured another significant victory at Chancellorsville, Virginia, in May 1863. Just a few months later, however, the fortunes of war turned in the North's favor.

On July 4, 1863, Grant cleared a path through Mississippi for Union forces with a victory at Vicksburg. On the same day, General George Meade's Army of the Potomac defeated General Lee's Virginians at Gettysburg, Pennsylvania. The dual Union triumphs marked the beginning of the end for the Confederacy.

Not long after, Grant produced another victory at Chattanooga, and President Lincoln promoted him to lieutenant general. Lincoln summoned Grant to Washington, D.C., as general in chief of all the Union forces. After the president told Grant to devise a strategy to end the war, he started to slowly but surely destroy his Confederate foes.

Grant suffered heavy losses in the Battle in the Wilderness and in Spotsylvania, Virginia. However, he began to surround Lee's forces in Petersburg. Grant captured Richmond on April 3, 1865, and Lee himself surrendered to Grant at Appomattox Court

House on April 9. Meanwhile, Union forces under the command of General William T. Sherman had marched through Georgia. General Joseph E. Johnston surrendered to Sherman at Durham Station, North Carolina, on April 26.

After this series of Union victories, the war ended. In total, it had cost 600,000 American lives. Old-style battle tactics had not yet adjusted to the effectiveness of improved modern weaponry. Outdated formations were quickly chewed up by rapid-firing rifles and cannon. Though the human cost was great, President Lincoln and the Union Army had saved the nation and rid the land of slavery.

THE HUMAN WALL

In July 1861, 30,000 Union troops under the command of General Irvin McDowell marched toward the Confederate capital of Richmond, Virginia. Strong Confederate resistance led by Generals Pierre Beauregard and Joseph E. Johnston stalled McDowell's advance in the First Battle of Bull Run, causing McDowell to attempt a maneuver toward his enemy's west flank. As the Union forces tried to move, General Thomas J. Jackson's Virginia brigade held firm. After seeing this fierce fighting, another Confederate general, Barnard Bee, rallied his own Virginia brigade. He compared Jackson to a stone wall because he would not allow his troops to budge. The Southerners forced the army to pull back. Both Jackson and his brigade kept the name "Stonewall" for the rest of the war.

BLADES AND HORSES

Around the same time as the Civil War, military technology was experiencing major leaps forward. Advances were producing better weaponry, which both sides used to deadly effect. The Union and the Confederacy both used the rifle musket as the basic infantry weapon. It fired a Minié ball: a tapered, lead projectile. Steel bayonets came in two types—socket or sword. A socket bayonet fit around the front of the muzzle of the rifle. It measured 14 to 18 inches (36 to 46 cm) long. A sword bayonet had a handle and was shaped like a real sword. It could be attached to the side of the barrel of the rifle and extended well beyond the muzzle.

Though the early army was not known for excellent horsemanship, cavalry units became a significant force during the Civil War. Soldiers on horseback were armed with sabers, carbines (short rifles), and pistols. The cavalry's most valuable—and expensive—resource was the horse itself. Cavalrymen typically had to supply their own horses. If a horse was killed or wounded in action, the government would have to pay for a replacement.

RESTORING THE UNION

After the Civil War, Congress reduced the million-man Union Army to a U.S. Army that numbered just under 30,000 by 1871. The army took on new noncombat duties as occupation forces in the South. Soldiers were also used to suppress strife in industrial areas. The army was the only federal group with enough men to carry out the tasks of repairing infrastructure in the South.

The army's main focus during the Reconstruction era was peacekeeping. Its many other duties included civil matters, such as regulating commercial law, civil court proceedings, and public education. It also helped people become registered voters, ensured that former Confederate states could hold fair elections, and approved new state constitutions. The army was also kept busy as it helped the South literally rebuild. Soldiers also helped banks and railroads operate, and dealing with corrupt politicians and petty criminals was all part of the job.

Of all the army's important new functions during Reconstruction, perhaps the most crucial was protecting the rights of newly freed Black Americans. Though true racial equality would not begin to appear for many years, the Union Army's victory in the Civil War helped usher in a new era for the formerly enslaved people.

THE TIDE RISES

In the late 1860s, the U.S. government began to abandon its earlier policy of treating much of the West as a large Native American reserve. Instead, the government slowly but surely introduced a policy of confining Native Americans to small tribal reservations as settlers took the land. The Native Americans had little choice; they could accept the reservations, or they could fight.

Some tribes, such as the Crow of Montana and the Pueblo of the Southwest, agreed to life on the reservation. Others chose the path toward battle. Those who resisted included the western Sioux, Cheyenne, Arapaho, Kiowa, and Comanche on the Great Plains. They were joined by the Bannock and Nez Percé in the northern Rockies. The Apache spread terror across the Southwest. Once again, the U.S. Army was called to action. The government ordered the army to round up and force the warring tribes onto reservations. Not long after the Civil War, a final war to "win" the West commenced. Battles continued through the 1870s and 1880s.

Though Native Americans emerged victorious in a few scattered battles, they did not win a single campaign. Their most notable victory came at the Battle of the Little Bighorn in 1876. About 2,000 Sioux and Cheyenne, led by Chiefs Crazy Horse and Sitting Bull, wiped out an entire battalion of Colonel George Armstrong Custer's 7th Cavalry Regiment.

The series of isolated battles and full-scale conflicts between the army and Native Americans from 1865 to 1890 became known as the Indian Wars. Clashes raged over the plains, mountains, and deserts of the American West. The fighting was guerrilla-style, characterized by skirmishes, pursuits, raids, massacres, expeditions, battles, and campaigns. Each varied in size and intensity.

At this time, army soldiers included two infantry and two cavalry regiments of troops made up of Black Americans. The Native Americans they were fighting called them "buffalo soldiers," since they saw a similarity between the curly hair and dark

General Custer and his soldiers put up a courageous defense at the Battle of the Little Bighorn despite the overwhelming strength of their Native American opponents.

skin of the soldier and the buffalo. The army also employed a few Native American scouts, but by and large, white soldiers filled most of the enlisted ranks. Many were recent arrivals from Europe.

Since the days of the American Revolution, weapons had evolved. Basic army weaponry during the Indian Wars included single-shot Springfield and seven-shot Spencer rifles, Springfield carbines, Colt .45-caliber revolvers, sabers, Gatling guns, and

12-pound howitzers. A new firepower invention, the Gatling gun was a ten-barrel, crank-turned weapon capable of firing 400 rounds per minute. Howitzers could lob just two shells a minute, and they were not known for accuracy, but they made a lot of noise and had an undeniably destructive impact. On occasion, howitzers even helped the army drive off superior numbers of Native Americans.

Though the army had devastating and powerful weaponry, the Native Americans were formidable foes. They fought a fast-moving war, with their cavalry covering ground at amazing speeds. However, they fought in vain against the unstoppable rising tide of the westward expansion of the United States. The Indian Wars ended in South Dakota at a place called Wounded Knee on December 29, 1890. More than 30 army soldiers and 200 Lakota Sioux died in that final battle.

STILL MORE CONFLICT

The U.S. Army closed out the violent 19th century by participating in the Spanish-American War in 1898. Tensions between the United States and Spain began to rise when Cuba began its War of Independence against Spain in 1895. American leaders felt that Spanish influence so close to home was a threaten to U.S. security. As a measure of caution, President William McKinley sent the battleship USS *Maine* to protect American interests in Cuba.

On February 15, 1898, while sitting at the harbor at Havana, Cuba, the *Maine* exploded for unexplained reasons. Without proof, the United States immediately blamed Spain for the *Maine*'s explosion. Congress demanded that Spain immediately withdraw from Cuba. Spain replied by declaring war on the United States. In April, Americans went to war.

As it had in the past, the army significantly increased from its peacetime size (about 25,000 in this case) to a much larger number (about 300,000). President McKinley quickly ordered actions against the Spanish colonies of Cuba, Puerto Rico, and the Philippine Islands. U.S. Army and Navy forces defeated the Spaniards on every front. American soldiers marched into Manila in the Philippines in August 1898. It was the last offensive action of the war.

After Spain's defeat in this conflict—and the signing of the Treaty of Paris in 1898—the country gave up its claims on Cuba. It also handed Guam, Puerto Rico, and the Philippines over to U.S. control. Though the combined might of the army and navy had pushed back the Spanish, American soldiers now had to spend four years dealing with a revolt in the Philippines, a nation that eventually gained independence in 1946. With the close of another century, the U.S. Army had done its job to make the nation a military force worthy of respect around the world.

CHAPTER 3

THE TWO WORLD WARS

The face of full-scale fighting was unrecognizable less than 50 years from the conclusion of the Civil War. The days of soldiers firing single-shot weapons had almost vanished; modern warfare at the turn of the 20th century was ruled by fully automatic machine guns, huge artillery pieces, and seemingly invincible tanks. When European countries experienced unrest in the 1910s, the United States tried to stay out of it. Its efforts failed, and the army was once more called in to use new technology to its fullest wartime potential.

ALLIED AND CENTRAL POWERS AT WAR

As the flames of war began to engulf Europe, the continent's nations split into two armed alliances. Great Britain, France, and Russia comprised the primary Allied Powers, or the Allies. On the other side were Germany and Austria-Hungary—the Central Powers—who aggressively attacked the Allies. Britain and France held back an initial German advance into France in the First Battle of the Marne in September 1914. The war, formerly centered around quick movement and high mobility, settled into a static trench war for the next two and a half years.

Because weapons had evolved more quickly than defensive technology, World War I was a conflict defined by its trench battles.

After handling so many armed conflicts in the 1800s, Americans did not want to go back to war. The nation had been following a policy of neutrality, meaning that it would generally not interfere in the affairs of other nations. However, Germany was conducting unrestricted submarine warfare by the year 1917, and a German U-boat (a type of submarine) sank the ship the *Lusitania*, with Americans aboard. Though President Woodrow Wilson had originally supported neutrality, he changed his mind. In early, 1917, he told Congress that Germany's new policy threatened U.S. ships and lives. Less than a week after Wilson's request, the United States declared war on Germany.

Before entering the conflict in Europe, there had been a lot of spending in preparation for potential war. Congress allotted funds for defense. The army bought modern rifles (the Springfield Model 1903), artillery, and field telephones. Units began experimenting with machine guns, aircraft, and other transport options. Structurally, the army established the nation's first peacetime divisions. These were self-contained and supporting fighting units of about 10,000 men each.

The army also explored new ways of rapidly expanding its ranks—both regular and National Guard—with well-trained personnel. (The National Guard had risen out of state militias in the decade after the Civil War.) The Reserve Officer Training Corps (ROTC) was also starting to be created during this time. Despite these efforts, the army remained unprepared for the type of conflict that World War I presented.

To bolster the ranks, President Wilson called for a draft. The Selective Service draft quickly grew the peacetime army. It grew from about 100,000 regulars to a wartime army of almost 4 million men in about a year and a half. General John J. Pershing was named to head the American Expeditionary Force (AEF) that would be fighting in Europe. The AEF set off for France on June 14, 1917.

CHANGING THE WAR

American soldiers saw limited action in their first war year. British and French leaders wanted to blend the U.S. troops into their own divisions, but General Pershing wanted to keep his AEF together. Pershing planned for the AEF to fight as an American army.

In late 1917, a revolution within Russia forced the country to make its own peace with Germany. The end of hostilities with Russian soldiers freed German troops for use in the West. In 1918, Germany launched a series of offensives, beginning in March and ending unsuccessfully in mid-July.

Americans joined the battle in May. It soon became obvious that they were not ready for the fight. Though the United States was a leading industrial nation at the time, army soldiers went to war using many British and French weapons, some of which were unreliable. Despite equipment shortcomings, army troops impressed their veteran German foes with their raw courage and ability to adapt.

Germany's offensive campaign ended in the Second Battle of the Marne on July 17, 1918. As in 1914, the Marne River was the key location of the battle. The next day, Allied forces launched their own series of counteroffensives. Steady Allied advances restored most of France and Belgium by October. British, Belgian, French, and American victories across a wide front led to the treaty that ended World War I in 1919.

Pershing's First and Second Armies were major players in the final Allied offensive in the Meuse-Argonne. Six other American divisions led the way for Allied offensives elsewhere. The AEF's initiative and added numbers tipped the balance of power toward the Allies. By working closely together—relying often on the U.S. Army—the Allied Powers won the war. However, peace was never a long-term option.

TROUBLE IS BREWING

The Treaty of Versailles, signed in 1919, formally brought an end to World War I. Germany was forced to accept the blame for Allied losses and to pay huge fines and penalties for the war it created. The treaty also reduced and restricted the size of Germany's land and military. These terms were harsh, intended to prevent Germany from ever becoming strong enough to wage another war. However, they

DOWNSIZING

After World War I, the U.S. Army was quick to cut back spending. It returned to a peacetime, all-volunteer force of just over 220,000 men. Congress authorized the establishment of a voluntary training program for an expanded National Guard and an organized reserve, but kept tight control on other military funding. The army soon did not have enough money to construct a modern armored force. By the mid-1930s, it could not field a single combat-ready division.

also produced an economic depression, leading to a bitterness among the German people.

In the 1920s, German dictator Adolf Hitler gained power and attacked the Treaty of Versailles as an unfair punishment to the German state. Hitler's rapid rise was fueled by widespread German unhappiness, and by the 1930s, war was already on the horizon.

Across the ocean, war was looking more and more likely by 1935. Congress gradually increased the U.S. Army's size—just as a precaution—and in 1936, the army adopted the .30-caliber Garand (M1) semiautomatic rifle to replace the 1903 Springfield. Also during the 1930s, the mobile 105-mm howitzer was developed; it would become the army's primary big gun of World War II.

The army also designed and built light and medium tanks. It acquired new vehicles of various kinds. Motor power began to replace horses. In the midst of all this advancement, the army reduced the size of an infantry division to three regiments (from four). The smaller divisions improved the mobility of the newly mechanized army.

PUTTING NEW WEAPONS TO WORK

World War II began in Europe in September 1939 when Germany's Wehrmacht (armed forces) invaded Poland. Just as in World War I, Americans initially wanted no part of another European war. When Germany defeated France in 1940, however, alarm bells sounded in the United States. Britain now stood alone as the only obstacle between Americans and Hitler's new European fighting force.

Though the United States did not want to enter another war in Europe, it was soon impossible to ignore the crimes committed by Germany's Adolf Hitler.

As the conflict spread in Europe, Congress further expanded U.S. regular forces. The government planned to create a better-armed field force of 1.5 million by mid-1941. It also made the National Guard a federal force, called up the reserves, and initiated the draft.

In March 1941, Congress authorized a new program to send war supplies, including weapons and other equipment, to Britain. In return, Britain allowed the United States to set up military bases on British territories in the Western Hemisphere.

In June 1941, after Hitler's forces invaded the Soviet Union, the United States expanded its program to include selling to the Soviets. These actions were clearly not the act of a truly neutral nation, and they pushed the United States closer to war. However, the tipping point for American involvement came in an unexpected way.

AN INFAMOUS ATTACK

World War II suddenly struck the United States on December 7, 1941, when Japanese aircraft launched a sneak attack on U.S. naval installations in Pearl Harbor, Hawaii, and the Philippines. With hundreds of Americans dead and the navy weakened, the United States wasted little time declaring war on Japan. In response, Japan's ally—Germany—declared war on the United States. American soldiers weresoon thrust into war against the Axis Powers of Germany, Italy, and Japan.

Great Britain and the United States again became allies. They agreed to target Germany first, planning to hold things steady against Japan in the Pacific until victory was won in Europe. Japanese victories in the Pacific required more Allied attention than first anticipated, but the strategy stayed mostly on track.

The U.S. Army—made mostly of draftees—established itself as a powerful and flexible war force in World War II. The army at its height included more than 8 million officers and enlisted men. It fielded nearly 100 combat divisions, supported by a large tactical and strategic air force. The army also maintained many other service organizations that helped it wage a global war. American soldiers again fought bravely and effectively in a variety of environments.

Under the leadership of General Dwight D. Eisenhower, the U.S. Army began its ground campaign against Germany in November 1942. Allied forces drove Field Marshal Erwin Rommel's Armeegruppe Afrika (Army Group Africa) out of North Africa. Though many Americans were untested before the war, they learned to quickly mature in battle. Allied armies swept across Sicily and through Italy in 1943 and 1944, leading to Italy's defeat by 1944.

On June 6, 1944, the Allies landed in Normandy, France, to start their long march west to Berlin, Germany's capital. At the same time, Soviet forces advanced toward Germany from the eastern front. Less than a year later, the German government unconditionally surrendered to the Allies, marking

Dwight D. Eisenhower, who achieved incredible success in World War II, is another army general who would go on to become president of the United States.

an end to World War II in Europe. Now, attention could be focused on Japan.

Beginning at a small island called Guadalcanal in 1942, the United States had launched a two-pronged attack against Japanese forces in the Southwest and Central Pacific. General Douglas MacArthur commanded U.S. Army and Allied operations in New Guinea and the Philippines. Admiral Chester W. Nimitz directed U.S. naval forces in an island-hopping campaign that took them all the way through the Central Pacific. The twin offensives finally merged at the Japanese-held island of Okinawa, where U.S. forces defeated a stubborn enemy to win the last major battle of World War II.

The fighting officially ended on July 2, 1945, but it did not appear that the Japanese would surrender. On August 6, 1945, a U.S. B-29 bomber dropped the first ever atomic bomb, called Little Boy, on the Japanese city of Hiroshima. Three days later, another B-29 dropped another atomic bomb, called Fat Man, on the Japanese city of Nagasaki. The bombs totally destroyed both cities. On August 11, the Soviets entered the war against Japan, forcing Japanese leaders to formally surrender to the Allies in early September.

Just as it had done following the recent past wars, the U.S. Army began to shrink itself back down after World War II. Personnel numbers dropped and spending was slashed as the U.S. economy started to boom. After two global conflicts in less than 50 years, people were ready to see an end to armed fighting.

However, it soon became clear that the U.S. Army would still have to battle to defend the nation, this time in a different variety of conflicts.

TO HELL AND BACK

One of the army's most famous heroes, Audie Leon Murphy was the most decorated American soldier of World War II. Born in 1924 in Texas, he enlisted in the army in 1942. As a corporal, he fought across North Africa and up the Italian peninsula with the 3rd Infantry Division. From there, the 3rd landed on the beaches of southern France.

During his first action in France, Murphy earned the Distinguished Service Cross by wiping out a German machine gun nest. He earned a Purple Heart near Besançon in September, and two Silver Stars on October 2 and 5. A week later, he was promoted to the rank of second lieutenant. In late October, a sniper's bullet (for which he earned another Purple Heart) put him in the hospital for two months.

In early 1945, Murphy was given command of the 3rd's Company B, 1st Battalion, 15th Infantry Regiment. Near Colmar, he single-handedly fought off a German infantry company and six Tiger tanks. Facing the assault, Murphy ordered his company to withdraw while he stayed behind to cover their retreat. After jumping on a burning tank destroyer, he opened fire on the advancing Germans with a large-caliber machine gun. The attack stopped after 50 Germans died. Murphy received the Medal of Honor—among his 37 total decorations—for his heroism. After the war, Murphy described his wartime experience in a book titled *To Hell and Back*, and he enjoyed a successful career as a movie actor.

CHAPTER 4

CONFLICT OF A DIFFERENT KIND

After living through two brutal wars in the first half of the 1900s, people around the world wanted to find a way to achieve peace. The United Nations (UN) was founded in San Francisco in 1945 in an attempt to keep world affairs in order. However, it was not long after the end of World War II that the Soviet Union and the United States—former allies and two of the founding nations of the UN—developed an aggressive rivalry. Already uncertain about the economic idea of communism, Americans grew increasingly nervous as the Soviet Union expanded in Europe. The Cold War (named because the sides never openly fought) was the result of these increased tensions in the 1960s, and its effects would stretch for decades.

PREPARING FOR AN INTERVENTION

In 1949, a group of 12 Western powers formed a military alliance. Their shared aim was to defend Western Europe against potential Soviet expansion. Called the North Atlantic Treaty Organization (NATO), its most powerful members were the United Kingdom, France, Canada, and the United States. Each nation was committed to the cause, and if any country were to be attacked, the others would immediately rush to its defense. NATO's main goal was to discourage Soviet aggression.

NATO was formed by powerful Western countries to combat a growing Communist threat.

Though it was thousands of miles away, the United States was now resolved to defend Western Europe. Even so, the army cut back from 8 million men and nearly 100 divisions in 1945 to less than 600,000 men and 10 divisions in 1950. The Soviet Union first openly tested an atomic bomb in 1949, raising already high tension levels.

In 1950, the U.S. Army was on the march to war again—not in Europe, this time, but in Asia. Following World War II, the United States and the Soviet Union both had troops occupying Korea. They divided Korea into two temporary zones at the 38th parallel (a measure of latitude). Later attempts to reunite the divided country did not have success. North of the dividing line, Koreans adopted a Communist government; in the south, a democratic government rose to power. War erupted when North Korean president Kim Il-Sung attempted to reunite Korea by force, invading his southern neighbor. The United Nations and the United States intervened on behalf of South Korea.

President Harry Truman appointed General Douglas MacArthur as supreme commander of UN forces in the region. American troops began sailing from Japan to South Korea in July. This quick response reflected how seriously the United States took this action.

Despite a rapid show of force, the North Korean armies were able to drive the UN forces to the southern tip of the Korean peninsula. On July 29, U.S. Eighth Army commander General Walton H. Walker issued an order to his 25th Division that they must hold their ground or die trying. This division, and the UN forces, held the line at the Pusan Perimeter.

General MacArthur then conducted a seaborne landing at the city of Inchon with army and marine forces. His brave action cut the North Korean invaders off. MacArthur then chased their fleeing armies northward to the Chinese border. In an unanticipated response, China entered the war and drove the UN forces back below the 38th parallel.

Not unlike the conditions of World War I, the Korean War devolved into trench warfare. UN forces fought along a main line of resistance and at outposts in front of the lines. They were using mostly outdated weapons from World War II. In the skies, however, new P-80 Shooting Stars and MiG-17 jets saw combat for the first time. By 1953, both sides agreed to stop fighting, though neither admitted defeat. North and South Korea became separate nations, but a true final ending to the war has never been reached.

The U.S. Army played a major part in the Korean War, and many Americans made sacrifices to protect the country from a Communist takeover. The Korean War Veterans Memorial features 19 stainless steel statues representing the U.S. soldiers who fought in the war.

A COLD COLD WAR

After the Korean War, President Dwight D. Eisenhower adopted a new policy for defense, focusing on nuclear deterrence. Instead of serving on the fighting fronts, the U.S. Army assumed a secondary role of handling small international conflicts. However, presidents John F. Kennedy and Lyndon B. Johnson moved away from an aggressively nuclear policy. They worked to restore the army as the nation's first line of armed defense in Europe. Both Kennedy and Johnson also called on the army to combat Communist uprisings in smaller countries. Vietnam became the focus of this policy.

In 1954, the Communist forces of Ho Chi Minh defeated the French in the First Indochina War. Afterward, Vietnam was divided, awaiting the results of free elections in 1956. Ho Chi Minh decided to reunite the country by force. Supported by the Soviet Union, his Vietcong fighters started a guerrilla war in South Vietnam in 1959.

In response, Kennedy sent more than 15,000 military personnel to help South Vietnam. These troops included Green Beret Special Forces and advisers. After Kennedy's assassination in November 1963, President Lyndon Johnson continued sending support troops to South Vietnam.

The Tet Offensive of 1968 marked a major a turning point in the war. After a series of battles, U.S. forces dealt a great military defeat to the Vietcong. Back in the United States, however, Americans had

MAKING A RESOLUTION

Early in August 1964, North Vietnamese patrol boats attacked U.S. Navy destroyers in the Tonkin Gulf. President Johnson asked Congress to grant him expanded powers to defend the United States. On August 7, the Senate approved the Tonkin Gulf Resolution by a vote of 88 to 2. The House of Representatives passed it by a voice vote of 416 to 0.

During the next six months, Vietcong guerrilla fighters attacked several American bases in South Vietnam. In each attack, Americans died. President Johnson started to rapidly deploy additional U.S. forces to South Vietnam. They eventually numbered more than half a million.

come to oppose the war on both practical and political terms. President Johnson switched to a strategy that would wind the war down. Though Johnson did not seek reelection, new president Richard M. Nixon supported his idea of exiting the Vietnam War. Nixon worked out a ceasefire agreement and U.S. troops withdrew from Vietnam in 1973.

Without U.S. support, the South Vietnamese army was finally defeated after a 1975 North Vietnamese offensive. The war ended in a Communist victory. Vietnam was officially reunited in 1976 as the Socialist Republic of Vietnam. Nearly 60,000 Americans died in the Vietnam War.

MODERNIZATION IN THE LATE 20TH CENTURY

During the war in Vietnam, the army tested new weapons in combat. Helicopters saw use as both troop transports and fire support. Air-based tactics emerged and were developed. The army acquired new tanks and armored vehicles. It adopted the M14 and M16 rifles and the M79 grenade launcher. Its divisions were reformed into three brigades. Importantly, the Vietnam War also saw the first actions of Green Beret Special Operations Forces.

The U.S. Army's Green Berets were first deployed for operations late in the Vietnam War.

BRANCHES AND RESPONSIBILITIES

Marines and army soldiers performed similar duties in Vietnam, but their strategies differed. Both services conducted ground operations to search out and destroy enemies and enemy bases. After engaging the enemy, army units would return to base and await the next operation. Marines, on the other hand, favored a technique called the "enclave strategy." Using this approach, marines would occupy and defend important geographic areas and military installations. By holding strategic points, the marines hoped to free South Vietnamese forces for inland operations. The strategy was meant to keep the South Vietnamese army as a key contributor to the war effort. In the end, neither strategy succeeded.

The U.S. Army entered the Vietnam War at the peak of training and administrative efficiency. Years of difficult overseas fighting wore down its manpower and spirit. The army became a shell of its earlier combat effectiveness. Discipline and leadership weakened. Racial violence and drug abuse grew rampant. Attacks on officers and noncommissioned officers increased in Vietnam and around the world.

President Nixon called for an end to the draft in 1973. In addition to the army's other problems, it now faced a new labor challenge. The army only pulled itself back together thanks to the help of a strong core of dedicated leaders. The army reinvented itself in the two decades after the Vietnam War as an all-volunteer fighting force.

In the 1980s, Congress approved large military budgets under President Ronald Reagan. The army developed and bought new weapons and equipment. It revamped its training programs to prepare soldiers for highly mobilized, fast-moving air and land warfare. This new training was meant to help win a war against a similarly equipped Soviet army. However, that clash of superpowers never happened. In 1991, the collapse of the Soviet Union ended the Soviet threat and the Cold War. The new army's first major engagement would come in the Middle East.

OPERATIONS IN THE DESERT

In August 1990, the Iraqi forces of dictator Saddam Hussein invaded the tiny nation of Kuwait. The United States and its UN allies fought against the invaders as part of the Persian Gulf War. Led by the United States, the coalition began a military buildup in the Gulf area. This prewar phase was called Operation Desert Shield. At the same time, peace talks failed to convince Saddam Hussein to withdraw his troops from Kuwait.

In late 1990, President George H. W. Bush warned Saddam that the United States was ready for full-scale conflict. Bush ordered Saddam to withdraw by January 15, 1991, or face removal by force. Saddam did not comply. In response, Bush ordered an all-out air assault on Iraq and the Iraqi troops in Kuwait just one day after his deadline. So began Operation

Desert Storm, the most violent phase of the Persian Gulf War.

With new weapons, training, and strength, the U.S. armed forces put an end to the war in less than two months. Army soldiers and marines engaged in a ground attack in March 1991, and in less than a week, Saddam Hussein declared that he would remove his troops from Kuwait. This marked the end of the Persian Gulf War and demonstrated to the world that though the U.S. Army had taken a physical and spiritual beating in the late 20th century, it was once again on top.

Operation Desert Storm gave the United States the opportunity to show off the new and improved army.

CHAPTER 5

AN ATTACK ON AMERICAN SOIL

September 11, 2001, is one of the darkest days in U.S. history. In a coordinated attack, foreign extremists hijacked and crashed two planes into the Word Trade Center towers in New York City, killing thousands of Americans on U.S. soil. These terrorists, as they became known, also took control of two other planes, crashing one into the Pentagon; the other eventually crashed in a Pennsylvania field. American intelligence officers soon discovered that a wealthy Saudi Arabian named Osama bin Laden was responsible for organizing a terrorist group called al-Qaeda to carry out the attacks. The United States moved quickly to seek this group out and protect Americans at home and abroad from a new breed of threat.

DOMESTIC PROTECTION

President George W. Bush quickly formed the Office of Homeland Security. He charged the new agency with many tasks, including improving intelligence and security. Bush wanted to protect Americans, especially on U.S. soil. The nation's armed forces were critical to his plans. Operation Noble Eagle was born from the ashes of the September 11 attacks.

Established immediately after the September 11 attacks, the Department of Homeland Security has taken on many anti-terrorist responsibilities.

Noble Eagle is the name for U.S. military operations in homeland defense. More than 35,000 service personnel have answered the call for help, including thousands of new recruits to the National Guard. Troops from this branch helped out during the recovery effort in New York City after the attacks. Guardsmen and women were among the first on the scene.

Service members also lend their aid during other crises. Their uses include fighting forest fires and controlling civil unrest, such as riots. When needed, they provide disaster relief for floods and hurricanes. Their assistance during hurricanes Katrina and Rita in 2005 and Hurricane Harvey in 2017 helped save American lives.

Under the umbrella of Noble Eagle, one key army mission has been increasing airport security. Soldiers also stand guard at dams, power plants, and military bases. They also protect valuable infrastructure, including tunnels, bridges, rail stations, and emergency command posts.

STARTING IN AFGHANISTAN

After establishing the Department of Homeland Security, Bush's next actions were focused on the offensive. On September 25, 2001, Secretary of Defense Donald Rumsfeld kicked off Operation Enduring Freedom. It was his name for America's war on terrorism. Under Enduring Freedom, the

U.S. Army was sent to war in Afghanistan. (The army now also fights terrorism in other countries.)

Al-Qaeda, the organization behind the September 11 attacks, had cells in dozens of countries, but because it was based in Afghanistan, that nation became the obvious first target for the United States. Al-Qaeda and the Taliban regime controlled 80 percent of the country. The Northern Alliance held the remaining 20 percent. United States Central Command—overseeing conflicts in the Middle East, East Africa, and Central Asia—was responsible for the situation in Afghanistan.

Right after the September 11 attacks, President Bush met with his top advisers. During the conference, General Hugh Shelton, chairman of the Joint Chiefs of Staff, ordered Tommy Franks, leader of Central Command, to devise a strategy for dealing with Afghanistan.

Franks quickly responded with three options. The first proposed a basic cruise missile strike. It would target al-Qaeda training camps and Taliban military bases. The second added manned bombers—B-1s and B-52s—to option one. The third called for cruise missiles, manned bombers, and soldiers to be physically present to fight. Central Command and Secretary Rumsfeld went for option three. Special Operations Forces were identified as the most qualified troops for ground operations. Other U.S. Army and Marine units would be called on as needed. Planning for the operation continued around the clock. Action in Afghanistan was set to begin on October 7, 2001.

Army general Tommy Franks took charge of the new "war on terror" in Afghanistan.

A huge air bombardment kicked off the Afghan War. Bombs and missiles took out targets across the breadth of Afghanistan. Cities targeted in the attack included Herat in the west, Kandahar in the south, Kabul and Jalalabad in the east, and Mazar-e-Sharif in the north. These important targets were destroyed. Soon after, American boots hit the ground. U.S. Special Operations Forces linked up with Northern Alliance units in late October.

Though the army had been using advanced vehicles for decades, Special Operations Forces troops often rode horses into battle. Afghanistan is full of mountains, unpaved roads, and rocky trails. Even the impressive Humvees could not freely move within the rugged country as easily as horses. Special Operations Forces soldiers worked in small teams of 5 to 12. They wore winter uniforms that were half-American and half-Afghan. Some grew bushy beards, helping them blend in with their Afghan comrades of the Northern Alliance.

In early November, Alliance fighters began a full-scale assault on Mazar-e-Sharif, the northern stronghold of al-Qaeda and the Taliban. Special Forces called in air strikes. This important city fell two days later. A chain reaction followed, and all the major Afghan cities surrendered in quick succession. Kunduz followed Herat, Kabul, and Jalalabad. The last Taliban bastion at Kandahar fell in early December.

On December 22, 2001, the Afghans set up an interim government. Leaders placed Hamid Karzai at this government's head. Osama bin Laden

SPECIAL OPERATIONS IN ACTION

Central Command's plan called for the Afghans themselves to play a leading role in removing Taliban rule. Franks wanted the people to help rebuild their government on a solid foundation. Special Operations Forces were intended to provide guidance and support.

Special Operations Forces carried custom radios and Global Positioning System (GPS) beacons. They were capable of directing close air support and pinpointing air-attack targets. These elite troops also provided command assistance. Their duties included gathering intelligence, and they were also called into combat when needed.

remained at large, but Afghans now held the key to their future in their own hands. In the bigger picture, Central Command had only just begun to work in the Middle East.

WIDENING THE NET

Near the end of 2001, President Bush summoned Franks to his Texas ranch. Over the course of the following year, Central Command made major alterations to its Iraq strategy, hoping to improve its effectiveness.

On March 20, 2003, Baghdad citizens awakened to the cry of air raid sirens just after 5:30 in the morning. Bursts of red and yellow tracer shots streaked the city's dark sky, searching for an unseen enemy. The crash of bursting anti-aircraft shells joined the sirens in a song of destruction. Moments later, cruise missiles and precision bombs rained down on the city. Huge explosions rocked the earth. Smart munitions sought their targets: Iraqi dictator Saddam Hussein and his top supporters.

Less than an hour later, President Bush appeared on television at the White House. It was just after 10:00 pm in Washington, D.C. The president announced the start of the U.S. air attack on Baghdad. The first major war of the new century had officially begun.

An alliance of armed forces from the United States, Great Britain, Australia, and Poland opened up war with Iraq for a second time. There were three significant causes of the Iraq War. First, the allied nations thought Saddam Hussein had weapons of mass destruction, including nuclear and biological weapons. Second, alliance countries believed that he was connected to terrorists working against the West. Third, they considered Saddam Hussein and his government to be a threat to his neighbors and to a region in dire need of stability. Since the early 1990s, Saddam Hussein had repeatedly ignored UN actions and orders arising from the Persian Gulf War.

It remains unclear whether these reasons made the Iraq War a justified military action. A more complete judgment must await the test of time. Regardless, the performance of U.S. Army soldiers and their allies is clear: they carried out their missions with dedication and precision.

In March 2003, U.S. and British forces launched a ground assault from Kuwait into Iraq. The next day, U.S. aircraft began an intense bombardment of Baghdad and other targets. The deadly air attack was meant to "shock and awe" Iraqi commanders into giving up. Over the next three weeks, American soldiers and marines quickly covered the 350 miles (563 kilometers) from Kuwait to downtown Baghdad.

About 10,000 vehicles and more than 15,000 soldiers moved up the Euphrates River. The U.S. Army's 3rd Infantry Division led the western arm of a twin American offensive. U.S. Marines of the First Marine Expeditionary Force covered the 3rd Division's right flank, advancing up the Tigris River.

Special Forces troops took control of two key airfields in the west. Soldiers of the 82nd and 101st Airborne Divisions and the 173rd Airborne Brigade fought smaller battles on the way to the Iraqi capital. Special Forces and their Kurdish allies pressed down from the north. British troops assaulted Basra in the south. In less than a month, Saddam Hussein's brutal administration was ended, as was the major combat in the Iraq War.

In April 2003, Franks held a press conference from one of Saddam's palaces in Baghdad. He announced an official end to the most violent phase of the fighting in Iraq. Once again, the U.S. Army had proven the quality of an all-volunteer army supported by solid funding and advanced technology.

THANKS TO THE TANKS

Today, the U.S. Army ranks among the fastest, most powerful fighting forces in history. It owes much of its mobility and strength to the M1 Abrams main battle tank. Regarded as one of the world's best weapons, the heavily armored M1 Abrams weighs 63 tons (57 mt). Despite its weight, its maximum speed is 45 miles (72 km) per hour. Not very fuel efficient, the tank uses almost 2 gallons (7.5 L) of gas to cover a single mile. Its weapons include a 120 mm gun, a .50-caliber machine gun, and two .30-caliber machine guns. It comes equipped with thermal imaging, night vision, laser range finders, and computerized targeting. All things considered, the M1 Abrams is one of the most technologically advanced war machines ever.

The M1 Abrams is one of the most destructive and feared military vehicles in the world.

CHAPTER 6

A STRONG, DIVERSE ARMY

Any organization can be made stronger by embracing diversity of races, beliefs, orientations, and backgrounds. The U.S. Army is no exception. Though its history of inclusion has not always been progressive, the modern U.S. military understands that its units are stronger when soldiers come from many walks of life. As part of its ongoing commitment to improving its strength, the army is always striding forward to become more accepting.

A HISTORY OF EXCELLENCE

Black Americans have served with honor in all of the wars in which the United States has ever fought. Black soldiers participated in state militias during colonial conflicts. During the American Revolution, they fought at Lexington and Concord. Black Americans later served at Bunker Hill, New York, Trenton, Princeton, Savannah, Monmouth, and Yorktown.

After the American Revolution, the army cut back its forces. Until the Civil War, nearly every soldier was a white man. On January 1, 1863, President Abraham Lincoln delivered a speech called the Emancipation Proclamation to free enslaved people. Lincoln opened enlistments in the Union Army to Black men. Nearly 200,000 Black soldiers fought for their freedom in 39 major battles and 449 separate actions. The Medal of Honor was awarded to 18 Black soldiers.

After the Civil War, Congress added four Black regiments to the ranks of the army. These groups served primarily in the West. In 1877, Henry Ossian Flipper became the first Black man to graduate from West Point and the first Black soldier to receive an officer's commission. Black soldiers went on to serve in the Spanish American War. They also fought in the Philippines and on the Mexican Punitive Expedition of 1916.

World War I struck during a time of increased segregation, when rights for Black Americans were being slowly taken away again. Black leader W. E. B.

In the face of discrimination and hardship, activist and leader W. E. B. Du Bois suggested that Black Americans could earn respect through army service.

Du Bois encouraged Black men to serve in the military. He argued that service to the country would help people win back their rights. Nearly 400,000 Black soldiers served in the army during World War I. Many fought in eight segregated combat regiments.

Though Black soldiers served well in the war, the army cut all Black infantry regiments after World War I. It also excluded Black soldiers from new specialties, such as aviation. The army pushed to use Black Americans only as laborers in future wars. By 1940, only 5,000 Black soldiers and 5 Black officers remained in the army. However, when World War II began, the army again turned to Black Americans to fill its ranks. Despite facing continued discrimination in the military, they answered the call.

Nearly a million Black soldiers served in the armed forces in World War II. Black men and women served mostly in segregated units. Many were found in the ranks of motor transport and support units. A handful of Black Americans were allowed to take flight training at the Tuskegee Institute in Alabama. They gained fame as pilots known as the Black Eagles.

In 1948, President Harry Truman issued Executive Order 9981. His goal was to force the military to end its longstanding practices of segregation for people of color. At first, the army was slow to act on the order. After suffering heavy combat losses in Korea in 1951, the army was forced to take action. It began mixing Black soldiers into formerly all-white units. Though this was a step in the right direction, Black officers still numbered only about 3 percent of the army's officer corps.

At the height of the Vietnam War, Black Americans represented 11 percent of the U.S. population. They were extremely well represented in the military, accounting for 12.6 percent of the American troops in Vietnam. Most Black soldiers served in the infantry, and many were draftees. Black soldiers made up nearly 15 percent of all U.S. combat casualties in the war. Countless Black soldiers became unsatisfied. Many banded together as brothers suffering from the same discrimination.

HIGH-RANKING BLACK LEADERS

After President Nixon ended the draft in 1973, Black Americans were more interested in enlisting. Toward the end of the 20th century, Black Americans made up one-third of the army's soldiers, and its officer corps was 10 percent Black. In 1977, Clifford Alexander became the first Black secretary of the army. In 1989, President George H. W. Bush named General Colin Powell as chairman of the Joint Chiefs of Staff, making him the first Black American to hold that office.

Powell's policies reduced the size of the military at the end of the Cold War while maintaining the stature of the United States as a global power. He played a major role in the Persian Gulf War in 1991, advocating overwhelming force to achieve quick victory. His aggressive tactics during Operation Desert Storm contributed to the quick victory. Powell's vision and use of the chairman's authority helped shape a modern U.S. Army for its role in a modern world.

In today's army, Black soldiers enjoy more equality than ever before. The army can still improve its racial affairs, but it has made great strides in achieving racial justice. In addition, today's army also leads the way in gender issues.

SEIZING RESPONSIBILITY

Women have served in the U.S. Army going all the way back to the American Revolution. For two centuries, women served most commonly as supporters

A decorated soldier and excellent leader, Colin Powell became the first Black man to be the chairman of the Joint Chiefs of Staff.

of men who saw combat duty. A few women disguised as men fought in the 1700s and 1800s. In World War I, more than 20,000 women served in the Army Nurse Corps. Others filled clerical positions at home. However, the first large-scale recruitment of women did not occur until World War II. Army chief of staff General George C. Marshall opened the door to women taking on more responsibilities in the military.

On May 14, 1942, the Women's Auxiliary Army Corps (WAAC) was formed. Its name was changed to the Women's Army Corps (WAC) in 1943. Colonel Oveta Culp Hobby served as the first director of the WAAC and WAC. About 100,000 found a home in the WAC, which the army used to fill support roles to free men for combat. Despite the wartime push, the role of women in the army almost disappeared after World War II.

In 1948, Congress passed the Women's Armed Services Integration Act, allowing women to become permanent members of the armed services for the first time. Initially, the army only permitted women to serve in noncombat specialties. It also limited overall numbers to 2 percent of active-duty personnel. Female officers could not advance beyond the rank of lieutenant colonel. In the 1970s, women pushed for and achieved more opportunities. Poor enlistment numbers and calls for equal treatment drove improvements. Among the victories was the removal of a rank ceiling, as female officers could now become generals.

Some enhancements came along with the end of the draft and the start of the all-volunteer policy. The army recruited more females to offset an expected reduction of male enlistments. Women were allowed to command mixed units of both men and women. Mixed training of male and female recruits began. The benefits offered to married male and female soldiers were made equal. Women who became pregnant no longer faced an automatic discharge. Women began pilot training in 1974, and the doors to West Point opened to them in 1976.

Female soldiers made the best of their new opportunities. Women took part in every major

There have been thousands of female graduates from West Point since women were first allowed to attend the school in 1976.

troop deployment during the 1990s, serving in Panama's Operation Just Cause and Operations Desert Shield and Desert Storm in Iraq. Today, women make up 15 percent of the armed services. They serve in all kinds of specialties. Many of them are combat-related, and a new 2017 policy has opened the door to allowing women to serve on the front lines, which had previously been forbidden.

MORE ORIENTATION ACCEPTANCE

The history of gay men and women who want to serve in the military has always been mixed. In the past, all services have discharged gay servicemen and women if their orientations became known. Between 1941 and 1996, more than 100,000 gay soldiers were discharged across all service branches. Even officers were not immune to this unfair policy.

In 1973, gay men and women began to challenge these discriminatory practices in court. The Department of Defense responded by issuing Directive 1332.14 in 1981. The order doubled down on the discharge of gay people from the military. President Bill Clinton tried to overturn the policy in 1993. He wanted to allow gay men and women to openly serve. Gay opponents resisted. Public Law 103-160 attempted to reach a compromise. The compromise was called the "don't ask, don't tell" (DADT) policy.

The DADT policy required gay men and women in the military to conceal their orientation. As long as they lived and served in silence, commanders were instructed not to look into their sexuality. The armed forces continued to grapple with this situation, discharging another 10,000 gay soldiers. Meanwhile, gay men and women were still forced to conceal their identities if they wanted to serve their nation.

On December 15, 2010, the House of Representatives voted to repeal DADT by passing bill H.R. 2965. Three days later, the Senate followed suit by passing bill S. 4023. President Barack Obama signed the repeal into law on December 22, 2010. The DADT policy was officially removed on September 20, 2011, allowing gay men and women to serve without fear of losing their jobs because of their orientation.

Many important steps have been taken toward achieving equality in race, gender, and orientation. However, the modern U.S. Army can still improve. There is still work to be done to make the army more inclusive, but leaders at the top are making an effort every day. As opportunities continue to arise for people of color, females, and members of the LGBTQ+ community—and capable soldiers seize those responsibilities—the army moves closer to real equality.

CHAPTER 7

RANKS AND RESERVES

More than anything, the U.S. government is responsible for protecting its nation and its citizens. The area of the federal government that oversees this responsibility is the Department of Defense, led by the secretary of defense (a person appointed by the president). All of the major armed service branches—U.S. Army, Navy, Air Force, Marines, and Coast Guard—report to the Department of Defense. At a lower level, the U.S. Army is broken into two important groups: active duty soldiers and reserve soldiers. Those on active duty are deployed around the world to serve at international bases and conduct missions as assigned. Those in reserve—as members of the Army Reserve and Army National Guard—are not full-time soldiers, but they are still ready to be deployed at a moment's notice if directed to do so.

STARTING FROM THE TOP

Standing at the top of the army chain of command is the president of the United States, who also has the title of commander in chief. This means that the president is directly in charge of every military action taken by the country. Just below the president is the secretary of defense, who oversees the secretary of the army. Next down is the chief of staff of the army, who supervises the Department of the Army Headquarters (HQDA) staff and directly reports to the secretary of the army. Three Army Commands (ACOM), nine Service Component Commands (ASCC), and eleven Direct Reporting Units (DRU) report to the HQDA staff.

Each ACOM is in charge of assigned units and facilities. The army also includes six geographic Areas of Responsibility (AORs), known as Unified Commands. Three additional Unified Commands support those that are assigned to AORs: Special Operations Command (SOCOM), Strategic Command (STRATCOM), and Transportation Command (TRANSCOM).

In the language of military organization, any unit larger than a corps is called an army. Depending upon the scope and size of an operation, an army has three levels of descending size: army group, theater army, and field army.

An army group is made up of two or more field armies. It is the largest ground formation used in combat operations. Its commander is commonly a general or lieutenant general.

A theater army is the chief army element in a Unified Command. It oversees matters of operations and support. A theater commander directs it.

A field army consists of two to five corps. A corps itself contains two to five divisions. A division comprises three brigades, which consists of three or more battalions. Three to five companies make up a battalion. Each company contains three to four platoons made up of three to four squads. A squad, the smallest tactical unit, consists of four to ten soldiers.

The U.S. Army has not deployed a unit as large as an army group since World War II. Even in Operation Desert Storm—a huge show of military force—General H. Norman Schwarzkopf commanded a field army. During Operation Iraqi Freedom, General Tommy Franks did not command anything larger than a corps. The army currently maintains three field armies—the First, Third, and Fifth.

The U.S. Army rarely deploys soldiers in massive groups, but General Schwarzkopf was placed in charge of a field army during Operation Desert Storm.

WHAT'S THE JOB?

As viewed by the U.S. Department of Defense, the world is split into six geographic "Areas of Responsibility" (AOR), which are assigned to supervisory offices called Unified Commands. Unified Commands operate together with other agencies of the U.S. government and military partners from local nations. Though their physical locations are vastly different, the commands have a mutual mission to promote security and peaceful development in their AORs. The Unified Commands are:

- Africa Command (AFRICOM)—AOR: African nations not covered by CentCom

- Central Command (CentCom)—AOR: 25 countries in Northeast Africa; Southwest and Central Asia, including much of the Middle East; and the island nation of Seychelles

- European Command (EuCom)—AOR: All of Europe and parts of the Middle East

- Northern Command (NorthCom)—AOR: United States, its territories, and its interests related to homeland defense

- Southern Command (SouthCom)—AOR: 19 Central and South American countries (south of Mexico) and 12 Caribbean countries; adjacent waters, including the Gulf of Mexico and part of the Atlantic Ocean

- Pacific Command (PaCom)—AOR: 43 countries, 20 territories, and 10 U.S. territories; waters from the east coast of Africa to the west coast of the United States, and from the Arctic Ocean to the Antarctic Ocean

BATTLE BRANCHES

Overall, the U.S. Army should be considered as a fighting unit sworn to the defense of the United States. It draws on the military skills of five combat branches to fulfill this mission. They are infantry, artillery, armor, aviation, and the corps of engineers.

Infantry soldiers fight on foot, typically using only the weapons and ammunition they can carry. In modern times, the most basic weapon is the soldier's rifle. They can also use grenades, machine guns, mortars, and other special weapons. Handheld antitank weapons can lend an added boost in combat. The infantry's primary mission is to engage, destroy, or capture the enemy.

Artillery use in war dates back to machines that could throw rocks in an age before gunpowder. Today's artillery consists of large-caliber weapons with incredible destructive power. Artillery includes howitzers, cannons, and rockets. Many modern guns use computers to locate targets, and artillery is the unquestioned ruler of land combat.

Armor became a separate branch of the U.S. Army in 1950. Cavalry units merged with armor, and horses gave way to armored vehicles. Armor's vehicles of choice are the M1 Abrams main battle tank and the Bradley Fighting Vehicle. These powerful vehicles are supported by infantry, artillery, air power, and helicopters. Armor uses advanced maneuvers, protected firepower, and sheer shock to engage and destroy the enemy.

Artillery has been around since the days of cannons, and modern artillery pieces are incredibly powerful.

Army aviation was formed as a separate branch of the U.S. Army in 1983. It consists of aircraft that are needed for day-to-day ground operations. Such aircraft are overseen by a ground commander. Light planes are used for artillery spotting and observation duties. Helicopters serve as troop and cargo transports. Helicopters also serve as close fire-support weapons, heavy vehicle destroyers, and medical evacuation vehicles.

The corps of engineers is among the nation's oldest military units. It was founded in 1775 and now constructs roads, bridges, and bases to aid military operations. Engineers build forts and other defenses to protect troops and territory. The corps of engineers also constructs many civil works. These projects include building reservoirs, levees, dams, veterans' hospitals, post offices, and more.

WAITING IN THE WINGS

The Army Reserve and the Army National Guard lend additional support to U.S. Army missions. The Army Reserve was created by the National Defense Act of 1916 with a mission to provide the nation with trained and ready soldiers when needed. Reserve soldiers stand in the wings, awaiting their call to support national strategies at all times.

Today's Army Reserve consists of three levels of service: the Selected Reserve, the Individual Ready Reserve, and the Retired Reserve. More than a million reservists between these three divisions stand at the ready for the president's orders.

The Selected Reserve is the most generally available group of reservists. All Selected Reserve soldiers can be activated in an emergency. Up to 30,000 Individual Ready Reserve soldiers can also be called up. Many people in this group have left active duty, but they still have an obligation to serve in the Army Reserve.

Ready Reserve soldiers number well over 600,000 (including Army National Guard). Retired Reserve soldiers are closer to about 400,000. They are retirees from the Active Army, the Army Reserve, and the Army National Guard. Though they are sometimes considered "backups," Army Reserve soldiers have taken part in every U.S. military operation since 1990.

The Army National Guard is an elite group of citizens who are also soldiers. Guard members donate a portion of their time to serving their nation. Each state maintains its own National Guard, and each state's units are sworn to serve a dual purpose: protecting their state and protecting their nation. The National Guard provides states with units trained and equipped to protect life and property. It also stands ready to defend the United States and its interests around the world.

FROM CIVILIAN TO SOLDIER

Training is the official process by which the U.S. Army transforms civilians into soldiers. Reserve and National Guard soldiers generally train one weekend each month. They also take part in a two-week Field Training Exercise once a year. Because they are not actively deployed, Reservists and National Guardsmen and women dedicate only part of their time to the armed forces.

On the other hand, working in an active-duty position is a full time job. Enlisted army soldiers must take Basic Combat Training. They then move on to Advanced Individual Training in a military job specialty.

In addition to specialty education, the U.S. Army offers a wide range of training. Expanded training topics include tactical, technical, physical, and leadership development. Leadership training helps to turn good soldiers into good leaders. It teaches the skills needed to lead from the front. Unit training in drills and field exercises develops individual and team skills to keep soldiers sharp.

Young army soldiers who want to advance their careers even further can seek focused training in specialty schools. Qualified soldiers can receive training in such topics as aviation, medicine, law, information and communications, languages, music, recruiting, and more.

Warrior training offers tough but rewarding challenges. Ranger, Pathfinder, and Special Forces schools test the physical and mental skills of the army's finest soldiers. Army Rangers excel at leading soldiers on difficult missions. Pathfinders pave the way for airborne soldiers or army aircraft. Special Forces wage dangerous secret warfare all across the globe.

The broad range of army training helps to equip soldiers with the confidence and skills needed to take on almost any mission in life.

GETTING INTO TRADITION

One of the U.S. Army's greatest strengths is that its members are willing to put the team above themselves. To help recruits understand this change from their first day in the army, young soldiers are forced to adapt to new rules. They accept new duties. They develop new outlooks. Recruits embrace the traditions and practices that define the army way of life. General customs such as military discipline, courtesy, rank, and regulations lend order to daily routines. The army way of doing things soon becomes second nature to new soldiers-in-training.

As in all military forces, success in the U.S. Army is often tied to rank. Privileges increase as soldiers advance in rank. In today's fighting force, it is possible—though rare—for a recruit to start at the bottom and climb to the top of the career ladder, rising from private to general. A soldier who works hard and has a good attitude has no limits on how much they can achieve and succeed.

The training to become an Army Ranger is even more mentally and physically challenging than standard boot camp.

MILITARY DISCIPLINE

Military discipline describes reliable obedience among military personnel. It results from training. Repeated drills, such as gun drills, bayonet drills, and marching, help to instill it. Discipline is essential to an effective military unit. It is the glue that binds soldiers and their actions together.

Courtesy is an easy one: it is just polite behavior. Most civilian rules of courtesy apply to army life. Some courtesies are used only in military services. Officers are addressed as "sir" out of respect for their ranks. Hand salutes are performed before all higher officers and the American flag as it waves. Military courtesy encourages harmony between individuals from all walks of life.

The United States relies on its system of laws, rules, regulations, and procedures. The U.S. Army does too. The army's unique laws are established by Congress, the Department of Defense, the Department of the Army, and other lawmaking groups.

For nearly 200 years, from 1775 to 1950, the army abided by a set of laws known as the Articles of War. In 1950, Congress created a new military justice system called the Uniform Code of Military Justice (UCMJ). The UCMJ applies to all branches of the U.S. military and all members of the armed forces.

Military justice is similar to—and just as important—as criminal justice for civilians. Because members of the armed forces have so much responsibility, however, they have to follow some laws that are new or different. For example, mutiny (trying to take authority from the captain of a ship) and desertion (breaking a contractual obligation to serve in the military) are crimes unique to the UCMJ. Any soldier suspected of breaking a law is quickly arrested and placed under court-martial. Soldiers' cases are typically handled quickly, from investigation to enforcement. In this way, the UCMJ is often better than civilian criminal courts, where trials can drag on for months or years. Overall, military law under the UCMJ is the backbone of modern army life; it defines the rights, rules, and responsibilities for any U.S. soldier.

CHAPTER 8

CAREERS FOR TODAY—AND TOMORROW

Though a soldier's main job is often to suit up and fight, there is much more to a career in the U.S. Army than combat missions overseas. As part of the training process for recruits, the army offers education to get specially trained for more than 150 different jobs. These jobs range from administrative support to legal advisement, and these skills can help a soldier find great employment if and when they decide to retire from army service.

GETTING ON BOARD

All across the nation, the U.S. Army is trying to recruit. Army recruiters—special soldiers who are tasked with filling out the ranks—can help applicants decide which service option is best for them. Options include Army Active Duty, Army Reserve, National Guard, ROTC, and West Point. Each option has different requirements for qualification and completion.

Enlisted soldiers are the solid core of the army. They perform specific jobs and tasks to ensure the success of a mission. To enlist in the U.S. Army, an applicant must meet these requirements:

- Be at least 18 and not more than 35 years old
- Be able to pass a physical examination
- Be able to meet requirements for appropriate behavior and background
- Be able to qualify for enlistment based on the Armed Services Vocational Aptitude Battery (ASVAB)

The requirements for enlisting in the Army Reserve and National Guard are similar.

Officers are the army's managers. They possess the skills and training needed to inspire and encourage others. Officers provide leadership to enlisted soldiers in all situations. Because of this level of responsibility, there are additional requirements for becoming an officer:

- Applications from ROTC must be U.S. citizens who are accepted to or enrolled in a qualifying college or university
- West Point candidates must be at least 17 years old and not older than 23 by July 1 of the year of entering the academy. Admittance into West Point also has its own set of qualifications:
  - Must be a U.S. citizen at the time of admission
  - Must be unmarried and with no legal obligation to support a dependent
  - Must meet academic, physical, and medical requirements
  - Must be a high school graduate and submit SAT or ACT assessment results for evaluation
- Applicants must be nominated by a member of Congress or the secretary of the army. Secretary nominations are also permitted for enlisted personnel in the U.S. Army, the Army Reserve, or the Army National Guard, as well as for ROTC or JROTC cadets.

There are other ways to earn a commission, including the Army's Warrant Officer Candidate School, Officer Candidate School, and as a Direct Commission Officer.

ROTC can be a great option for a young person still on the fence about joining the army full-time.

GETTING COMPENSATED

Service in the U.S. Army is a highly beneficial option. The nation benefits by having a strong defense force. The military community benefits by gaining a new member. Not least, the individual serving and their family benefit from the generous compensation package. The army can provide a healthy lifestyle with a sense of purpose. The branch supports those who serve with an excellent benefits package, including:

- Comprehensive health care
- Food, housing, and education assistance
- Family services and support groups
- Special pay for special duties
- Generous time off
- Strong retirement plans

Of the total compensation package (i.e., salary plus benefits value) offered to army soldiers, more than half can be counted as benefits other than cash. Noncash benefits include health care, retirement pay, child care, and free or subsidized food, housing, and education. Active duty soldiers also earn basic pay, which is a set rate based on rank and seniority.

Enlisted soldiers may also earn supplemental pay for special duties, hardship duties, foreign language proficiency, flights, and diving and sea duties. Though actual amounts depend on the type of duty, this extra pay can be several hundred dollars per month. The army also pays reenlistment bonuses to those who continue to serve after their contract is up; these amounts vary, but can be in the tens of thousands of dollars.

PROVIDING FOR SOLDIERS AND FAMILIES

Today, the U.S. Army provides soldiers and their families with comprehensive health care, life insurance, and plenty of time off. Health care comes in the form of an HMO-type plan called TRICARE. This program provides medical and dental care at little or no cost, typically at a military treatment center. Other programs help soldiers and their families serving at remote sites or overseas. Service members' group life insurance provides soldiers and reservists with a selection of low-cost group life insurance.

Paid time off makes up an important part of a soldier's life and well-being. Soldiers on active duty earn 30 days of paid vacation annually. They commonly get off on weekends and holidays—except when duty intervenes. The army also provides sick days to soldiers as needed.

The army encourages and assists soldiers who want to attend college or take continuing education classes. Soldiers can take advantage of the Montgomery GI Bill (MGIB) to pay for a college education. By contributing a small amount each month during the first year of service, a soldier may receive more than $61,000 in total benefits to help pay for college, split up over a span of several years.

For those with existing student debt, the Army College Loan Repayment Program makes paying off student loans easier. Soldiers who serve for a set number of time—typically longer than three years—can claim thousands of dollars of repayment allowances. The Army Reserve and ROTC offer additional educational incentives.

The army also offers other services, support groups, counseling, and training for soldiers' entire families. Many of these benefits come for free or at discount prices. These services include relocation assistance and financial planning advice. Family advocacy services offer everything from new parent support to abuse prevention.

Legal Assistance Centers provide soldiers with advice on personal legal matters. Attorneys on staff can be used to review legal documents, such as contracts and leases, and prepare wills, official letters, and other documents. The centers also assist soldiers with free tax preparation and electronic filing.

The Mobilization and Deployment Support program provides pre-deployment and reunion briefings. The program helps soldiers and their families with a variety of topics related to life at home, such as managing a household budget and keeping up communication with deployed units.

For army soldiers with children, Child and Youth Services offers affordable child care programs. Costs are adjusted according to rank and pay grade. The

Army Morale, Welfare, and Recreation programs deliver a wide selection of recreation, sports, entertainment, travel, and relaxation activities for soldiers and their families, no matter where they serve.

CHOOSING THE ARMY LIFE

For active duty career soldiers, the army offers countless rewards, both monetary and otherwise. However, any young person considering enlistment should carefully weigh the costs of committing to an army career. Time is the first commitment. Both the Regular Army and the Army Reserve require a minimum enlistment time of two years. Enlisted soldiers and officers cannot quit the army because they had a bad day; they must honor the terms of their enlistment or service contracts.

Close to a million soldiers are committed to the defense of the United States. The army assigns about one quarter of them to direct combat jobs. These jobs involve serious risks, including potentially serious physical injury. There are also risks to mental health, such as post-traumatic stress disorder (PTSD). In the worst cases, combat can be life threatening.

There are also less obvious risks and downsides of an army life. The stress of overseas deployment and long separations from home and family can be difficult to handle. Separations can contribute to the development of personal and financial difficulties. Anyone thinking about joining the army should keep all this in mind.

DECORATIONS IN THE ARMY

Just by joining the U.S. Army, each soldier has already carried out a heroic act. However, some soldiers are presented with opportunities to exhibit their courage in combat or during other missions. The government gives awards and medals to those who have gone above and beyond the call of duty. Some army commendations are listed below:

Bronze Star: Awarded for combat bravery or worthy achievement, in or out of combat

Combat Infantryman Badge: Awarded to soldiers actively engaged in ground combat

Distinguished Service Cross: Awarded to soldiers who demonstrate bravery during combat, especially for heroism at the risk of life

Medal of Honor: Awarded to the best of the best soldiers who carry out heroic actions in combat

Purple Heart: Awarded for wounds received in action against an enemy

Silver Star: Awarded for gallantry less notable than that needed for a Distinguished Service Cross.

ALWAYS IMPROVING

Today's army is always working to improve itself and strengthen the future for the military branch. With a combination of advanced technology, strong tactical prowess, and great people filling its ranks, the army of the 21st century is among the greatest fighting forces ever created. To maintain the army's excellence, its vision for the future includes a global reach with regional focus. Working with other military branches, including the navy, troops can be transported from anywhere in the world *to* anywhere in the world. Additionally, soldiers stationed at local bases, such as in Japan, can quickly respond to threats nearby.

Soldiers form the backbone of the army vision. To succeed in its missions, the army has established a history of effective actions and strong values. Soldiers live the life, perform the deeds, and uphold the Warrior Ethos of the Army. Soldiers represent the nation's finest citizens—the best of the best.

From the ranks of selfless citizens, the army will continue to select and train leaders for this century and beyond. Its training programs will produce decisive, adaptive, innovative leaders. Officers will be educated in the art and science of a modern professional soldier. They will demonstrate outstanding character and integrity. Future young leaders will think creatively, pursue lifelong learning, and boldly face challenges and complex problems.

The lifestyle of an army soldier is unique. There is a certain structure to military service that simply does not exist in civilian life. Traditions and the UCMJ set out strict rules and regulations that must be followed at all times. Anyone who struggles with discipline and cannot listen to authority will not find much help in the army. However, anyone who can recognize the potential benefits and accept the risks of living as a soldier may find that the U.S. Army is an incredible opportunity to improve their life.

GLOSSARY

buffalo soldier American Indian name for an African American soldier serving in the western United States after the Civil War.

CentCom Central Command; one of several U.S. Unified/Joint Commands; oversees operations in Iraq.

ethos Guiding beliefs of a person, group, or institution.

GI American soldier; name derives from "government issue."

Hessians Eighteenth-century German auxiliaries contracted for military service by the British government.

Humvee High-mobility, multipurpose wheeled vehicle (HMMWV or Hummer).

M1 Abrams Main U.S. battle tank.

M16 U.S. 5.56 mm semiautomatic rifle.

militia A civil military force that supplements a regular army in an emergency.

minutemen During the American Revolution, militia members able to assemble under arms at a minute's notice.

Reconstruction Generally refers to the period in U.S. history immediately following the Civil War in which the federal government set the conditions that would allow the rebellious Southern states back into the Union.

Tonkin Gulf Resolution A joint resolution passed by the U.S. Congress in response to the Gulf of Tonkin incident, giving U.S. president Lyndon B. Johnson authorization for the use of "conventional" military force in Southeast Asia.

Wehrmacht German armed forces.

FOR MORE INFORMATION

Association of the United States Army
2425 Wilson Boulevard
Arlington, VA 22201
Website: www.ausa.org
Facebook: @AUSA.org
Instagram and Twitter: @AUSAorg
This nonprofit association was created to support U.S. Army soldiers—and their families—through education, professional development, and networking.

Go Army
Website: www.goarmy.com
Facebook, Instagram, and Twitter: @GoArmy
This official website has information about joining the army, including requirements and career paths open to recruits.

Military.com: Army
133 Boston Post Road
Weston, MA 02493
Website: www.military.com/army
Facebook, Instagram, and Twitter: @Militarydotcom
This website has entries on every branch of the U.S. armed forces, and its page on the army includes information on pay grades, army statistics, and more.

U.S. Army

4700 Knox Street
Fort Bragg, NC 28310
Website: www.army.mil
Facebook, Instagram, and Twitter: @USArmy
The official website of the U.S. Army contains news, history, and general information about the branch.

U.S. Department of Defense

1000 Defense Pentagon
Washington, DC 20301-1000
Website: www.defense.gov
Facebook, Instagram, and Twitter: @DeptofDefense
The official website of the Department of Defense provides breaking news articles about military action as well as links for more information about specific armed forces branches.

FOR FURTHER READING

Billings, Tanner. *The U.S. Army*. New York, NY: Rosen Publishing, 2021.

Blackmon, Jimmy F. *Ranger School: Discipline, Direction, Determination*. New York, NY: Knox Press, 2021.

Eason, Sarah. *Special Forces Careers*. New York, NY: Crabtree Publishing, 2021.

Farrell, Mary Cronk. *Standing Up Against Hate: How Black Women in the Army Helped Change the Course of WWII*. New York, NY: Abrams Books for Young Readers, 2019.

Garstecki, Julia. *Army Rangers*. Mankato, MN: Black Rabbit Books, 2019.

Goldsmith, Connie. *Women in the Military: From Drill Sergeants to Fighter Pilots*. Minneapolis, MN: Twenty-First Century Books, 2019.

Kirkman, M. *The Truth About Life as a U.S. Army Soldier*. North Mankato, MN: Capstone Press, 2020.

Mapua, Jeff. *Working with Tech in the Military*. New York, NY: Rosen Publishing, 2020.

Marx, Mandy R. *Amazing U.S. Army Facts*. North Mankato, MN: Capstone Press, 2017.

McCallum, Ann. *Women Heroes of the US Army: Remarkable Soldiers from the American*

Revolution to Today. Chicago, IL: Chicago Review Press, 2019.

Myers, Carrie. *Life in the U.S. Army*. San Diego, CA: BrightPoint Press, 2021.

Partridge, Elizabeth. *Boots on the Ground: America's War in Vietnam*. New York, NY: Viking, 2018.

Phillips, Howard. *Inside the Army Rangers*. New York, NY: PowerKids Press, 2022.

Russo, Kristin J. *Surprising Facts About Being an Army Soldier*. North Mankato, MN: Capstone Press, 2018.

Troupe, Thomas Kingsley, and Jomike Tejido. *The Tuskegee Airmen's Mission to Berlin*. North Mankato, MN: Picture Window Books, 2018.

INDEX

ABOUT THE AUTHOR

Eric Ndikumana is a former collegiate long-distance runner who has been living in Rochester, New York, since 2018. In his free time, he enjoys spending time outdoors, exploring new trails and parks with friends and family.

CREDITS

Designer: Michael Flynn; Editor: Siyavush Saidian